The scenery of mountains painted on the ever-changing azure canvas of the sky, the mysterious mechanism of the human body, the rose, the green grass carpet, the magnanimity of souls, the loftiness of minds, the depth of love—all these things remind us of a God who is beautiful and noble.

—Paramahansa Yogananda

~

THE PHOTOGRAPHS IN THIS CALENDAR are accompanied by selections from the writings of Paramahansa Yogananda, whose timeless and universal teachings have awakened many, of all races, cultures, and creeds, to a deeper awareness of the one reality that sustains and unites us all.

Whether spread over the vast heavens or hidden in the exquisite delicacy of a tiny flower, nature's beauty is always beckoning, inviting us to look behind the outward form and sense the presence of God within.

We hope that the thoughts and images in these pages will bring you inspiration and encouragement in the days and weeks of the coming year.

In this new year I am a new person. And I shall change my consciousness again and again until I have driven away all the darkness of ignorance and manifested the shining light of Spirit in whose image I am made.

– Paramahansa Yogananda

Sunrise, Lake of Two Mountains, Canada   Photograph by Robert Servranckx / Sojourns In Nature

December/January

29
monday

30
tuesday

31
wednesday

New Year's Day
1
thursday

Day After New Year's Day (N.Z.) *Bank Holiday (Scot.)*
2
friday

December 2008

s	m	t	w	t	f	s
	1	2	3	4	5	6
7	8	9	10	11	12	13
14	15	16	17	18	19	20
21	22	23	24	25	26	27
28	29	30	31			

3
saturday

January

s	m	t	w	t	f	s
				1	2	3
4	5	6	7	8	9	10
11	12	13	14	15	16	17
18	19	20	21	22	23	24
25	26	27	28	29	30	31

First Quarter ◐
4
sunday

January

5
monday *Paramahansa Yogananda's Birthday*

6
tuesday

7
wednesday

8
thursday

9
friday

10
saturday *Full Moon* ○

11
sunday

January

s	m	t	w	t	f	s
				1	2	3
4	5	6	7	8	9	10
11	12	13	14	15	16	17
18	19	20	21	22	23	24
25	26	27	28	29	30	31

February

s	m	t	w	t	f	s
1	2	3	4	5	6	7
8	9	10	11	12	13	14
15	16	17	18	19	20	21
22	23	24	25	26	27	28

Simplicity means to be free of desires and attachments, and supremely happy within.... It entails neither hardship nor deprivation, but the wisdom to work for and be content with what you truly need.

– Paramahansa Yogananda

Yuccas, White Sands National Monument, New Mexico   Photograph by Russ Burden

There is one Link, one Life eternal, which unites everything in the universe—animate and inanimate—one wave of Life flowing through everything.

— Paramahansa Yogananda

Sea turtles, Bora Bora, French Polynesia   Photograph by Michele Westmorland

January

12
monday

13
tuesday

14
wednesday

15
thursday

16
friday

January

s	m	t	w	t	f	s
				1	2	3
4	5	6	7	8	9	10
11	12	13	14	15	16	17
18	19	20	21	22	23	24
25	26	27	28	29	30	31

Last Quarter ◑

17
saturday

February

s	m	t	w	t	f	s
1	2	3	4	5	6	7
8	9	10	11	12	13	14
15	16	17	18	19	20	21
22	23	24	25	26	27	28

18
sunday

January

19
monday

Martin Luther King, Jr.'s Birthday (Observed)

20
tuesday

21
wednesday

22
thursday

23
friday

24
saturday

25
sunday

New Moon ●

January

s	m	t	w	t	f	s
				1	2	3
4	5	6	7	8	9	10
11	12	13	14	15	16	17
18	19	20	21	22	23	24
25	26	27	28	29	30	31

February

s	m	t	w	t	f	s
1	2	3	4	5	6	7
8	9	10	11	12	13	14
15	16	17	18	19	20	21
22	23	24	25	26	27	28

It is God's play of light and shadow that has made creation appear as it does to us. When you realize this, you see it as a dream motion picture.

— Paramahansa Yogananda

Monument Valley, Arizona   Photograph by Cheryl Opperman

A vast cosmos of the different forces of nature is tied together by God's directing power. Everything works in mutual harmony with the Divine Plan.

— Paramahansa Yogananda

Iceberg, Holkham Bay, Alaska   Photograph by John Hyde / AlaskaStock.com

January/February

26
monday

Australia Day (Aus.)

27
tuesday

28
wednesday

29
thursday

30
friday

31
saturday

1
sunday

January

s	m	t	w	t	f	s
				1	2	3
4	5	6	7	8	9	10
11	12	13	14	15	16	17
18	19	20	21	22	23	24
25	26	27	28	29	30	31

February

s	m	t	w	t	f	s
1	2	3	4	5	6	7
8	9	10	11	12	13	14
15	16	17	18	19	20	21
22	23	24	25	26	27	28

February

2
monday
First Quarter ◐

3
tuesday

4
wednesday

5
thursday

6
friday
Waitangi Day (N.Z.)

7
saturday

8
sunday

February

s	m	t	w	t	f	s
1	2	3	4	5	6	7
8	9	10	11	12	13	14
15	16	17	18	19	20	21
22	23	24	25	26	27	28

March

s	m	t	w	t	f	s
1	2	3	4	5	6	7
8	9	10	11	12	13	14
15	16	17	18	19	20	21
22	23	24	25	26	27	28
29	30	31				

Whatever path your heart's deep desire tells you to follow is your royal highway in this life, the route you should travel in order to reach the abode of lasting peace and happiness.

— Paramahansa Yogananda

Brown bears, Katmai National Park, Alaska   Photograph by Cheryl Opperman

Think of Divine Abundance as a mighty, refreshing rain; whatever receptacle you have at hand will receive it.

– Paramahansa Yogananda

Tulips in rain, Seabeck, Washington   Photograph by Don Paulson

February

9
monday
Full Moon ○

10
tuesday

11
wednesday

12
thursday
Lincoln's Birthday

13
friday

February

s	m	t	w	t	f	s
1	2	3	4	5	6	7
8	9	10	11	12	13	14
15	16	17	18	19	20	21
22	23	24	25	26	27	28

March

s	m	t	w	t	f	s
1	2	3	4	5	6	7
8	9	10	11	12	13	14
15	16	17	18	19	20	21
22	23	24	25	26	27	28
29	30	31				

14
saturday
St. Valentine's Day (U.S., Canada, and U.K.)

15
sunday

February

16
monday
Washington's Birthday (Observed) *Presidents' Day* *Last Quarter* ◑

17
tuesday

18
wednesday

19
thursday

20
friday

21
saturday

22
sunday

February

s	m	t	w	t	f	s
1	2	3	4	5	6	7
8	9	10	11	12	13	14
15	16	17	18	19	20	21
22	23	24	25	26	27	28

March

s	m	t	w	t	f	s
1	2	3	4	5	6	7
8	9	10	11	12	13	14
15	16	17	18	19	20	21
22	23	24	25	26	27	28
29	30	31				

Our thoughts are powerful creative forces floating in the ether ready to accomplish their purpose when they are concentrated and consciously directed.

— Paramahansa Yogananda

Lightning, Bryce Canyon, Utah   Photograph by Dave Welling

Burst that shell of "can't" into the free air of "I can."

– Paramahansa Yogananda

Sally Lightfoot crab, Galapagos National Park, Ecuador   Photograph by Mark and Leslie Degner

February/March

23
monday

24
tuesday

New Moon ●

25
wednesday

26
thursday

27
friday

28
saturday

February

s	m	t	w	t	f	s
1	2	3	4	5	6	7
8	9	10	11	12	13	14
15	16	17	18	19	20	21
22	23	24	25	26	27	28

March

s	m	t	w	t	f	s
1	2	3	4	5	6	7
8	9	10	11	12	13	14
15	16	17	18	19	20	21
22	23	24	25	26	27	28
29	30	31				

1
sunday

St. David's Day (Wales)

March

2
monday

3
tuesday

First Quarter ◐

4
wednesday

5
thursday

6
friday

7
saturday

Paramahansa Yogananda's Mahasamadhi

8
sunday

Daylight Saving Begins (U.S. and Canada)

March

s	m	t	w	t	f	s
1	2	3	4	5	6	7
8	9	10	11	12	13	14
15	16	17	18	19	20	21
22	23	24	25	26	27	28
29	30	31				

April

s	m	t	w	t	f	s
			1	2	3	4
5	6	7	8	9	10	11
12	13	14	15	16	17	18
19	20	21	22	23	24	25
26	27	28	29	30		

Unselfish sympathy is the bridge that connects each soul with other souls.

— Paramahansa Yogananda

Multnomah Falls, Oregon   Photograph by Dennis Frates

The surest sign of God's Presence is the burst of the dawn of peace, which is the first messenger to herald His secret approach.

– Paramahansa Yogananda

Sunrise, Torres del Paine, Chile   Photograph by Brian Luke Seaward

March

Sri Yukteswar's Mahasamadhi

9 monday

Full Moon ◯

10 tuesday

---

11 wednesday

---

12 thursday

---

13 friday

March

s	m	t	w	t	f	s
1	2	3	4	5	6	7
8	9	10	11	12	13	14
15	16	17	18	19	20	21
22	23	24	25	26	27	28
29	30	31				

14 saturday

April

s	m	t	w	t	f	s
			1	2	3	4
5	6	7	8	9	10	11
12	13	14	15	16	17	18
19	20	21	22	23	24	25
26	27	28	29	30		

15 sunday

March

16
monday

17
tuesday

St. Patrick's Day

18
wednesday

Last Quarter ◑

19
thursday

20
friday

Vernal Equinox

21
saturday

22
sunday

Mothering Sunday (Eng.)

March

s	m	t	w	t	f	s
1	2	3	4	5	6	7
8	9	10	11	12	13	14
15	16	17	18	19	20	21
22	23	24	25	26	27	28
29	30	31				

April

s	m	t	w	t	f	s
			1	2	3	4
5	6	7	8	9	10	11
12	13	14	15	16	17	18
19	20	21	22	23	24	25
26	27	28	29	30		

Only those who partake of the harmony within their souls know the harmony that runs through nature.

— Paramahansa Yogananda

Calla lily, Seabeck, Washington   Photograph by Don Paulson

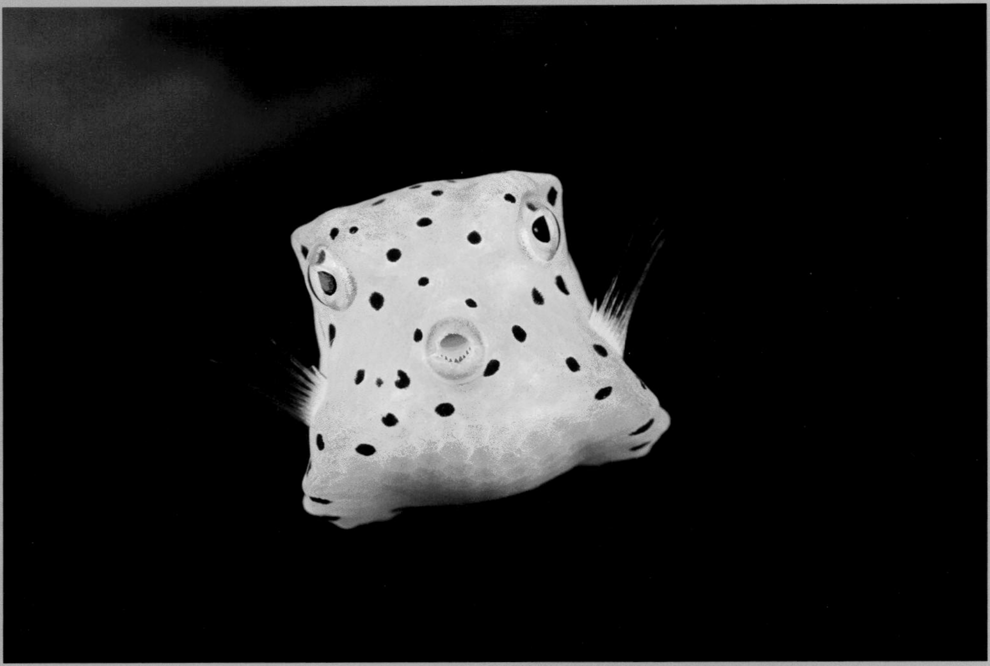

Let go and relax....When you are calm, you feel the whole universe of happiness rocking gently beneath your consciousness.

— Paramahansa Yogananda

Yellow boxfish, Indonesia   Photograph by Burt Jones and Maurine Shimlock

23
monday

24
tuesday

25
wednesday

New Moon ●

26
thursday

27
friday

March

s	m	t	w	t	f	s
1	2	3	4	5	6	7
8	9	10	11	12	13	14
15	16	17	18	19	20	21
22	23	24	25	26	27	28
29	30	31				

28
saturday

April

s	m	t	w	t	f	s
			1	2	3	4
5	6	7	8	9	10	11
12	13	14	15	16	17	18
19	20	21	22	23	24	25
26	27	28	29	30		

Daylight Saving Begins (U.K. and E.U.)

29
sunday

March/April

30
monday

31
tuesday

1
wednesday

2
thursday

First Quarter ◐

3
friday

4
saturday

5
sunday

March

s	m	t	w	t	f	s
1	2	3	4	5	6	7
8	9	10	11	12	13	14
15	16	17	18	19	20	21
22	23	24	25	26	27	28
29	30	31				

April

s	m	t	w	t	f	s
			1	2	3	4
5	6	7	8	9	10	11
12	13	14	15	16	17	18
19	20	21	22	23	24	25
26	27	28	29	30		

If we can learn to calm our mental waves of thoughts by the magic wand of concentration, then we will behold in our mental mirror our perfect, all-conquering soul ability.

—Paramahansa Yogananda

Cormorant fisherman, Li River, China Photograph by Cheryl Opperman

Walk surely on the garden path of life that leads to God, helping others along the way whom you find wandering by the wayside.

– Paramahansa Yogananda

Grape hyacinth and daffodils, Keukenhof Gardens, Netherlands   Photograph by Darrell Gulin

April

6
monday

7
tuesday

8
wednesday

Passover Begins *Full Moon* ○

9
thursday

Good Friday

10
friday

April

s	m	t	w	t	f	s
			1	2	3	4
5	6	7	8	9	10	11
12	13	14	15	16	17	18
19	20	21	22	23	24	25
26	27	28	29	30		

May

s	m	t	w	t	f	s
					1	2
3	4	5	6	7	8	9
10	11	12	13	14	15	16
17	18	19	20	21	22	23
24/31	25	26	27	28	29	30

11
saturday

Easter Sunday

12
sunday

April

13
monday

Easter Monday (All except U.S. and Scot.)

14
tuesday

15
wednesday

16
thursday

17
friday

Last Quarter ◑

18
saturday

19
sunday

April

s	m	t	w	t	f	s
			1	2	3	4
5	6	7	8	9	10	11
12	13	14	15	16	17	18
19	20	21	22	23	24	25
26	27	28	29	30		

May

s	m	t	w	t	f	s
					1	2
3	4	5	6	7	8	9
10	11	12	13	14	15	16
17	18	19	20	21	22	23
24/31	25	26	27	28	29	30

If you want to know God, you must be like the naughty baby who cries till mother comes.

— Paramahansa Yogananda

Gray wolf cubs in dandelions, Montana   Photograph by Daniel J. Cox, NaturalExposures.com

Try your utmost, and then try again....Then, out of the gloom of mysteries, the all-illuminating light of the Divine Guidance will emblazon your path.

– Paramahansa Yogananda

Del Norte Redwoods State Park, California   Photograph by Darrell Gulin

April

20
monday

21
tuesday

Earth Day

22
wednesday

St. George's Day (Eng.)

23
thursday

New Moon ●

24
friday

April

s	m	t	w	t	f	s
			1	2	3	4
5	6	7	8	9	10	11
12	13	14	15	16	17	18
19	20	21	22	23	24	25
26	27	28	29	30		

ANZAC Day (Aus. and N.Z.)

25
saturday

May

s	m	t	w	t	f	s
					1	2
3	4	5	6	7	8	9
10	11	12	13	14	15	16
17	18	19	20	21	22	23
24/31	25	26	27	28	29	30

26
sunday

April/May

27
monday

28
tuesday

29
wednesday

30
thursday

1
friday

First Quarter ◐

2
saturday

April

s	m	t	w	t	f	s
			1	2	3	4
5	6	7	8	9	10	11
12	13	14	15	16	17	18
19	20	21	22	23	24	25
26	27	28	29	30		

May

s	m	t	w	t	f	s
					1	2
3	4	5	6	7	8	9
10	11	12	13	14	15	16
17	18	19	20	21	22	23
24/31	25	26	27	28	29	30

3
sunday

Success…is a little seed-thought and you have to develop it.... All kinds of seeds of power are within you, waiting for you to develop them.

— Paramahansa Yogananda

Daylily stamens   Photograph by Therese Tusa / Rainbow

When the undulating waves of consciousness are stilled by yoga, the sage beholds in the inner calm the omnipresent Eternal Tranquility.

— Paramahansa Yogananda

Spring farmland, The Palouse, Washington   Photograph by Dennis Frates

May

May Day Bank Holiday (U.K. and Scot.)

4 monday

5 tuesday

6 wednesday

National Day of Prayer

7 thursday

Full Moon ◯

8 friday

May

s	m	t	w	t	f	s
					1	2
3	4	5	6	7	8	9
10	11	12	13	14	15	16
17	18	19	20	21	22	23
24/31	25	26	27	28	29	30

June

s	m	t	w	t	f	s
	1	2	3	4	5	6
7	8	9	10	11	12	13
14	15	16	17	18	19	20
21	22	23	24	25	26	27
28	29	30				

9 saturday

Sri Yukteswar's Birthday

Mother's Day (U.S., Canada, Aus., and N.Z.)

10 sunday

May

11
monday

12
tuesday

13
wednesday

14
thursday

15
friday

16
saturday

17
sunday

Last Quarter ◑

May

s	m	t	w	t	f	s
					1	2
3	4	5	6	7	8	9
10	11	12	13	14	15	16
17	18	19	20	21	22	23
24/31	25	26	27	28	29	30

June

s	m	t	w	t	f	s
	1	2	3	4	5	6
7	8	9	10	11	12	13
14	15	16	17	18	19	20
21	22	23	24	25	26	27
28	29	30				

The mother's love is not given to us to spoil us with indulgence, but to soften our hearts, that we may in turn soften others with kindness.

— Paramahansa Yogananda

Polar bear and cub, Manitoba, Canada   Photograph by Linda Drake

Perform all your duties with a courageous cheerfulness welling up from within you....You will see that a flood of vitality will move through all your muscles and through your entire body.

— Paramahansa Yogananda

Proxy Falls, Oregon   Photograph by Dennis Frates

May

18 monday

Victoria Day (Canada)

19 tuesday

20 wednesday

21 thursday

22 friday

23 saturday

May

s	m	t	w	t	f	s
					1	2
3	4	5	6	7	8	9
10	11	12	13	14	15	16
17	18	19	20	21	22	23
24/31	25	26	27	28	29	30

June

s	m	t	w	t	f	s
	1	2	3	4	5	6
7	8	9	10	11	12	13
14	15	16	17	18	19	20
21	22	23	24	25	26	27
28	29	30				

24 sunday

New Moon ●

May

25
monday

Memorial Day Spring Bank Holiday (U.K. and Scot.)

26
tuesday

27
wednesday

28
thursday

29
friday

30
saturday

First Quarter

31
sunday

May

s	m	t	w	t	f	s
					1	2
3	4	5	6	7	8	9
10	11	12	13	14	15	16
17	18	19	20	21	22	23
24/31	25	26	27	28	29	30

June

s	m	t	w	t	f	s
	1	2	3	4	5	6
7	8	9	10	11	12	13
14	15	16	17	18	19	20
21	22	23	24	25	26	27
28	29	30				

God doesn't readily respond to us, because we are shy before Him.... Don't be afraid of Him. Call Him your own and pursue Him unceasingly, in thought and in action, and you shall find Him to be the greatest haven of safety.

— Paramahansa Yogananda

African lion cub, Wildlife Waystation, California   Photograph by Dave Welling

When you increase your perception and feeling…you will automatically absorb truth from the book of nature.

— Paramahansa Yogananda

Waterfalls, Julia Pfeiffer Burns State Park, California   Photograph by Christopher Talbot Frank

June

Queen's Birthday (N.Z.)

1
monday

2
tuesday

3
wednesday

4
thursday

5
friday

June

s	m	t	w	t	f	s
	1	2	3	4	5	6
7	8	9	10	11	12	13
14	15	16	17	18	19	20
21	22	23	24	25	26	27
28	29	30				

6
saturday

July

s	m	t	w	t	f	s
			1	2	3	4
5	6	7	8	9	10	11
12	13	14	15	16	17	18
19	20	21	22	23	24	25
26	27	28	29	30	31	

Full Moon ○

7
sunday

June

8
monday

Queen's Birthday (Aus.)

9
tuesday

10
wednesday

11
thursday

12
friday

13
saturday

14
sunday

June

s	m	t	w	t	f	s
	1	2	3	4	5	6
7	8	9	10	11	12	13
14	15	16	17	18	19	20
21	22	23	24	25	26	27
28	29	30				

July

s	m	t	w	t	f	s
			1	2	3	4
5	6	7	8	9	10	11
12	13	14	15	16	17	18
19	20	21	22	23	24	25
26	27	28	29	30	31	

Calmness is the throne of God.

— Paramahansa Yogananda

Goldfinch and zinnias, Marion County, Illinois   Photograph by Richard Day / Daybreak Imagery

Yoga teaches you to look yourself honestly in the eye and find out what you are.

– Paramahansa Yogananda

Black-headed seagull, Nile Delta, Egypt Photograph by Jorge Rodrigues / AKM Images, Inc.

Last Quarter ◑

15
monday

16
tuesday

17
wednesday

18
thursday

19
friday

June

s	m	t	w	t	f	s
	1	2	3	4	5	6
7	8	9	10	11	12	13
14	15	16	17	18	19	20
21	22	23	24	25	26	27
28	29	30				

July

s	m	t	w	t	f	s
			1	2	3	4
5	6	7	8	9	10	11
12	13	14	15	16	17	18
19	20	21	22	23	24	25
26	27	28	29	30	31	

20
saturday

Father's Day (U.S., Canada, and U.K.) *Summer Solstice*

21
sunday

June

22
monday

New Moon ●

23
tuesday

24
wednesday

25
thursday

26
friday

27
saturday

28
sunday

June

s	m	t	w	t	f	s
	1	2	3	4	5	6
7	8	9	10	11	12	13
14	15	16	17	18	19	20
21	22	23	24	25	26	27
28	29	30				

July

s	m	t	w	t	f	s
			1	2	3	4
5	6	7	8	9	10	11
12	13	14	15	16	17	18
19	20	21	22	23	24	25
26	27	28	29	30	31	

The spiritual conqueror must advance boldly.

— Paramahansa Yogananda

Bull elk, Yellowstone National Park, Wyoming   Photograph by Cheryl Opperman

Establish your palace of peace on the rock of ages, the indestructible inner peace of God.

— Paramahansa Yogananda

Tower of Babel, Arches National Park, Utah   Photograph by Dave Welling

June/July

First Quarter ◐

29
monday

30
tuesday

Canada Day (Canada)

1
wednesday

2
thursday

3
friday

June

s	m	t	w	t	f	s
	1	2	3	4	5	6
7	8	9	10	11	12	13
14	15	16	17	18	19	20
21	22	23	24	25	26	27
28	29	30				

Independence Day

4
saturday

July

s	m	t	w	t	f	s
			1	2	3	4
5	6	7	8	9	10	11
12	13	14	15	16	17	18
19	20	21	22	23	24	25
26	27	28	29	30	31	

5
sunday

July

6
monday

7
tuesday

Full Moon ○

8
wednesday

9
thursday

10
friday

11
saturday

12
sunday

July

s	m	t	w	t	f	s
			1	2	3	4
5	6	7	8	9	10	11
12	13	14	15	16	17	18
19	20	21	22	23	24	25
26	27	28	29	30	31	

August

s	m	t	w	t	f	s
						1
2	3	4	5	6	7	8
9	10	11	12	13	14	15
16	17	18	19	20	21	22
23/30	24/31	25	26	27	28	29

In the spiritual life one becomes just like a little child—without resentment, without attachment, full of life and joy.

– Paramahansa Yogananda

Young red fox, Ontario, Canada   Photograph by Mike Grandmaison

Perfect balance is the altar of God.

– Paramahansa Yogananda

Balancing Rock, Guadalupe Mountains National Park, Texas   Photograph by Tim Fitzharris

July

13
monday

14
tuesday

Last Quarter ◑

15
wednesday

16
thursday

17
friday

July

s	m	t	w	t	f	s
			1	2	3	4
5	6	7	8	9	10	11
12	13	14	15	16	17	18
19	20	21	22	23	24	25
26	27	28	29	30	31	

18
saturday

August

s	m	t	w	t	f	s
						1
2	3	4	5	6	7	8
9	10	11	12	13	14	15
16	17	18	19	20	21	22
23/30	24/31	25	26	27	28	29

19
sunday

July

20
monday

21
tuesday

New Moon ●

22
wednesday

23
thursday

24
friday

25
saturday

Mahavatar Babaji Commemoration Day

26
sunday

July

s	m	t	w	t	f	s
			1	2	3	4
5	6	7	8	9	10	11
12	13	14	15	16	17	18
19	20	21	22	23	24	25
26	27	28	29	30	31	

August

s	m	t	w	t	f	s
						1
2	3	4	5	6	7	8
9	10	11	12	13	14	15
16	17	18	19	20	21	22
23/30	24/31	25	26	27	28	29

When the mind is calm, how quickly, how smoothly, how beautifully you will perceive everything!

— Paramahansa Yogananda

Sawtooth Wilderness, Idaho   Photograph by Christopher Talbot Frank

What tremendous intelligence is manifested in creation! The Infinite is working in everything.

— Paramahansa Yogananda

Cheetah, Kenya   Photograph by Denver Bryan / Kimballstock

July/August

27
monday

28
First Quarter ◐
tuesday

29
wednesday

30
thursday

31
friday

July

s	m	t	w	t	f	s
			1	2	3	4
5	6	7	8	9	10	11
12	13	14	15	16	17	18
19	20	21	22	23	24	25
26	27	28	29	30	31	

1
saturday

August

s	m	t	w	t	f	s
						1
2	3	4	5	6	7	8
9	10	11	12	13	14	15
16	17	18	19	20	21	22
23/30	24/31	25	26	27	28	29

2
sunday

August

3
monday

Summer Bank Holiday (Scot.)

4
tuesday

5
wednesday

Full Moon ○

6
thursday

7
friday

8
saturday

9
sunday

August

s	m	t	w	t	f	s
						1
2	3	4	5	6	7	8
9	10	11	12	13	14	15
16	17	18	19	20	21	22
23/30	24/31	25	26	27	28	29

September

s	m	t	w	t	f	s
		1	2	3	4	5
6	7	8	9	10	11	12
13	14	15	16	17	18	19
20	21	22	23	24	25	26
27	28	29	30			

Keep a secret chamber of silence within yourself, where you will not let moods, trials, battles, or inharmony enter.... In this chamber of peace God will visit you.

— Paramahansa Yogananda

Northrup Falls, Tennessee   Photograph by Byron Jorjorian / Photo Researchers, Inc.

Spiritual success comes by understanding the mystery of life; and by looking on all things cheerfully and courageously, realizing that events proceed according to a beautiful divine plan.

— Paramahansa Yogananda

Impala and lightning, Kenya   Photograph by Tim Fitzharris

August

10
monday

11
tuesday

12
wednesday

Last Quarter ◑

13
thursday

Janmashtami

14
friday

August

s	m	t	w	t	f	s
						1
2	3	4	5	6	7	8
9	10	11	12	13	14	15
16	17	18	19	20	21	22
23/30	24/31	25	26	27	28	29

15
saturday

September

s	m	t	w	t	f	s
		1	2	3	4	5
6	7	8	9	10	11	12
13	14	15	16	17	18	19
20	21	22	23	24	25	26
27	28	29	30			

16
sunday

August

17
monday

18
tuesday

19
wednesday

20
thursday

New Moon ●

21
friday

22
saturday

23
sunday

August

s	m	t	w	t	f	s
						1
2	3	4	5	6	7	8
9	10	11	12	13	14	15
16	17	18	19	20	21	22
23/30	24/31	25	26	27	28	29

September

s	m	t	w	t	f	s
		1	2	3	4	5
6	7	8	9	10	11	12
13	14	15	16	17	18	19
20	21	22	23	24	25	26
27	28	29	30			

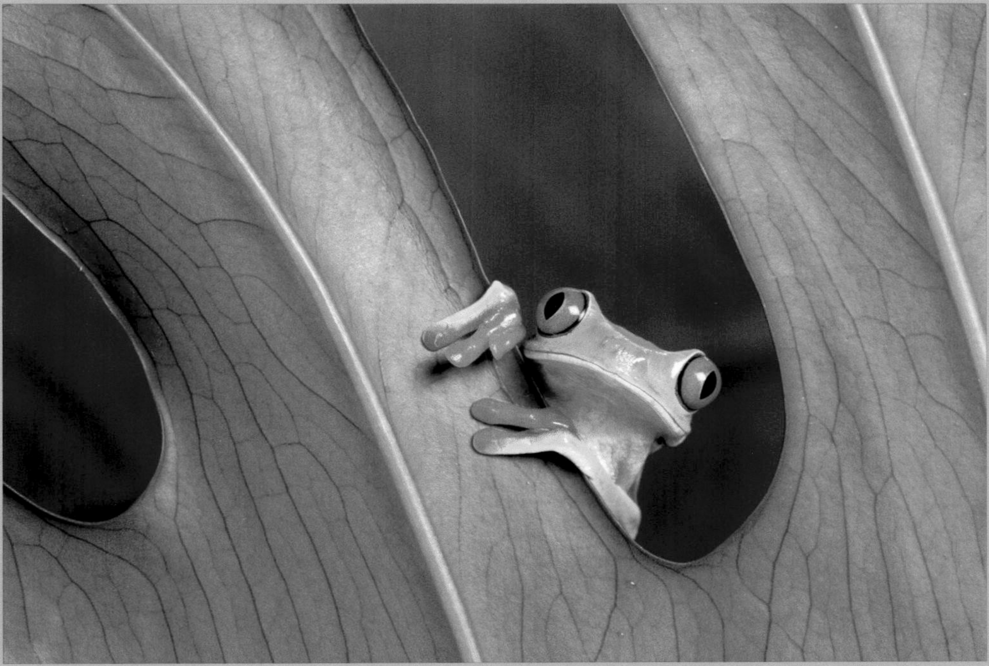

If you keep open your eyes of wisdom and calmness, you will see there is a lot of enjoyment in this world—just as though you are watching a motion picture.

— Paramahansa Yogananda

Red-eyed tree frog   Photograph by Klein and Hubert / BIOS / Peter Arnold, Inc.

Talk to God every second of your life.... He who is playing hide-and-seek in the beauty of the flowers, in souls, in noble passions, in dreams, shall come forth.

— Paramahansa Yogananda

Common vetch and Fairweather Range, Alaska   Photograph by Don Paulson

August

24
monday

25
tuesday

26
wednesday

First Quarter ◐
27
thursday

28
friday

August

s	m	t	w	t	f	s
						1
2	3	4	5	6	7	8
9	10	11	12	13	14	15
16	17	18	19	20	21	22
23/30	24/31	25	26	27	28	29

September

s	m	t	w	t	f	s
		1	2	3	4	5
6	7	8	9	10	11	12
13	14	15	16	17	18	19
20	21	22	23	24	25	26
27	28	29	30			

29
saturday

30
sunday

August/September

31
monday

Summer Bank Holiday (U.K. except Scot.)

1
tuesday

2
wednesday

3
thursday

4
friday

Full Moon ○

5
saturday

6
sunday

Father's Day (Aus. and N.Z.) *First Quarter* ◐

September

s	m	t	w	t	f	s
		1	2	3	4	5
6	7	8	9	10	11	12
13	14	15	16	17	18	19
20	21	22	23	24	25	26
27	28	29	30			

October

s	m	t	w	t	f	s
				1	2	3
4	5	6	7	8	9	10
11	12	13	14	15	16	17
18	19	20	21	22	23	24
25	26	27	28	29	30	31

Whether one acts quickly or slowly, in solitude or in the busy marts of men, his center should be peaceful, poised.

– Paramahansa Yogananda

Hippo and Lesser flamingos, Lake Nukuru, Africa Photograph by Darrell Gulin

Establish in yourself a temple of beauty and peace; there you will find God, on the altar of your soul.

— Paramahansa Yogananda

Japanese Garden, Portland, Oregon   Photograph by Dennis Frates

September

Labor Day (U.S. and Canada)

7
monday

8
tuesday

9
wednesday

10
thursday

Last Quarter ◑

11
friday

September

s	m	t	w	t	f	s
		1	2	3	4	5
6	7	8	9	10	11	12
13	14	15	16	17	18	19
20	21	22	23	24	25	26
27	28	29	30			

12
saturday

October

s	m	t	w	t	f	s
				1	2	3
4	5	6	7	8	9	10
11	12	13	14	15	16	17
18	19	20	21	22	23	24
25	26	27	28	29	30	31

13
sunday

September

14
monday

15
tuesday

16
wednesday

17
thursday

18
friday

New Moon ●

19
saturday

Rosh Hashanah

20
sunday

September

s	m	t	w	t	f	s
		1	2	3	4	5
6	7	8	9	10	11	12
13	14	15	16	17	18	19
20	21	22	23	24	25	26
27	28	29	30			

October

s	m	t	w	t	f	s
				1	2	3
4	5	6	7	8	9	10
11	12	13	14	15	16	17
18	19	20	21	22	23	24
25	26	27	28	29	30	31

The mysterious soul abides forever, changing never.... It loves to live in the grottos of change, ever steadfast and immovable. It never dreams aught but eternity.

— Paramahansa Yogananda

Ancient Anasazi granary, Grand Canyon, Arizona Photograph by JerryGinsberg.com

Learn to stand alone, secure in your own virtues and self-worth.

— Paramahansa Yogananda

Tricolored heron, Texas Photograph by Dave Welling

21
monday
U.N. International Day of Peace

22
tuesday
Autumnal Equinox

23
wednesday

24
thursday

25
friday
First Quarter ◐

26
saturday
Lahiri Mahasaya's Mahasamadhi

27
sunday

September

s	m	t	w	t	f	s
		1	2	3	4	5
6	7	8	9	10	11	12
13	14	15	16	17	18	19
20	21	22	23	24	25	26
27	28	29	30			

October

s	m	t	w	t	f	s
				1	2	3
4	5	6	7	8	9	10
11	12	13	14	15	16	17
18	19	20	21	22	23	24
25	26	27	28	29	30	31

September/October

28
monday

Yom Kippur

29
tuesday

30
wednesday

Lahiri Mahasaya's Birthday

1
thursday

2
friday

3
saturday

Full Moon ○

4
sunday

September

s	m	t	w	t	f	s
		1	2	3	4	5
6	7	8	9	10	11	12
13	14	15	16	17	18	19
20	21	22	23	24	25	26
27	28	29	30			

October

s	m	t	w	t	f	s
				1	2	3
4	5	6	7	8	9	10
11	12	13	14	15	16	17
18	19	20	21	22	23	24
25	26	27	28	29	30	31

If you have given up hope of ever being happy, cheer up. Never lose hope. Your soul, being a reflection of the ever joyous Spirit, is, in essence, happiness itself.

– Paramahansa Yogananda

Orangutan, Sacramento Zoo, California   Photograph by Tom and Pat Leeson / Kimballstock

Develop such mental power that you can stand unshaken, no matter what comes, bravely facing anything in life.

– Paramahansa Yogananda

Cape Kiwanda, Oregon   Photograph by Dennis Frates

October

5
monday

6
tuesday

7
wednesday

8
thursday

9
friday

October

s	m	t	w	t	f	s
				1	2	3
4	5	6	7	8	9	10
11	12	13	14	15	16	17
18	19	20	21	22	23	24
25	26	27	28	29	30	31

10
saturday

November

s	m	t	w	t	f	s
1	2	3	4	5	6	7
8	9	10	11	12	13	14
15	16	17	18	19	20	21
22	23	24	25	26	27	28
29	30					

Last Quarter ◐

11
sunday

October

12
monday

Columbus Day *Thanksgiving Day (Canada)*

13
tuesday

14
wednesday

15
thursday

16
friday

17
saturday

New Moon ●

18
sunday

October

s	m	t	w	t	f	s
				1	2	3
4	5	6	7	8	9	10
11	12	13	14	15	16	17
18	19	20	21	22	23	24
25	26	27	28	29	30	31

November

s	m	t	w	t	f	s
1	2	3	4	5	6	7
8	9	10	11	12	13	14
15	16	17	18	19	20	21
22	23	24	25	26	27	28
29	30					

Life is brief, yet it is unending. The soul is everlasting, but out of the short season of this life you should reap the most you can of immortality.

— Paramahansa Yogananda

Aspens and Wheeler Peak, Nevada Photograph by George Ward

Wisdom is the portal through which all races may pass into the one kingdom of truth.

— Paramahansa Yogananda

 Rainbow, Cypress River, Manitoba, Canada Photograph by Mike Grandmaison, www.grandmaison.mb.ca

October

19
monday

20
tuesday

21
wednesday

22
thursday

23
friday

24
saturday

First Quarter ◐ *Daylight Saving Ends (U.K. and E.U.)*

25
sunday

October

s	m	t	w	t	f	s
				1	2	3
4	5	6	7	8	9	10
11	12	13	14	15	16	17
18	19	20	21	22	23	24
25	26	27	28	29	30	31

November

s	m	t	w	t	f	s
1	2	3	4	5	6	7
8	9	10	11	12	13	14
15	16	17	18	19	20	21
22	23	24	25	26	27	28
29	30					

October/November

26
monday — *Labour Day (N.Z.)*

27
tuesday

28
wednesday

29
thursday

30
friday

31
saturday — *Halloween (U.S., Canada, and U.K.)*

1
sunday — *Daylight Saving Ends (U.S. and Canada)*

October

s	m	t	w	t	f	s
				1	2	3
4	5	6	7	8	9	10
11	12	13	14	15	16	17
18	19	20	21	22	23	24
25	26	27	28	29	30	31

November

s	m	t	w	t	f	s
1	2	3	4	5	6	7
8	9	10	11	12	13	14
15	16	17	18	19	20	21
22	23	24	25	26	27	28
29	30					

God's dream creation was not meant to frighten you, but to prod you to realize finally that it has no reality. So why be afraid of anything?

– Paramahansa Yogananda

Dead tree, Mt. Rainier National Park, Washington Photograph by Don Paulson / Jaynes Gallery

Just beneath the shadows of this life is God's wondrous Light.... When you meditate, you will find doors opening to Him everywhere.

– Paramahansa Yogananda

Big leaf maple trees, Monroe, Oregon   Photograph by Dennis Frates

November

Full Moon ○

2
monday

General Election Day

3
tuesday

4
wednesday

Guy Fawkes Day (Eng.)

5
thursday

6
friday

November

s	m	t	w	t	f	s
1	2	3	4	5	6	7
8	9	10	11	12	13	14
15	16	17	18	19	20	21
22	23	24	25	26	27	28
29	30					

7
saturday

December

s	m	t	w	t	f	s
		1	2	3	4	5
6	7	8	9	10	11	12
13	14	15	16	17	18	19
20	21	22	23	24	25	26
27	28	29	30	31		

Remembrance Sunday (U.K.)

8
sunday

November

9
monday

Last Quarter ◑

10
tuesday

11
wednesday

Veterans Day *Remembrance Day (Canada)*

12
thursday

13
friday

14
saturday

15
sunday

November

s	m	t	w	t	f	s
1	2	3	4	5	6	7
8	9	10	11	12	13	14
15	16	17	18	19	20	21
22	23	24	25	26	27	28
29	30					

December

s	m	t	w	t	f	s
		1	2	3	4	5
6	7	8	9	10	11	12
13	14	15	16	17	18	19
20	21	22	23	24	25	26
27	28	29	30	31		

Teach me to behold Thy face in the mirror of my stillness within.

— Paramahansa Yogananda

Prusik Peak, Washington Photograph by Jon Cornforth

A calm person, by the virtue of his self-possession, is always at peace with others, always happy, always calm.

– Paramahansa Yogananda

Mandarin duck, Littleton, Colorado   Photograph by Russ Burden

November

New Moon ●

16
monday

17
tuesday

18
wednesday

19
thursday

20
friday

November

s	m	t	w	t	f	s
1	2	3	4	5	6	7
8	9	10	11	12	13	14
15	16	17	18	19	20	21
22	23	24	25	26	27	28
29	30					

21
saturday

December

s	m	t	w	t	f	s
		1	2	3	4	5
6	7	8	9	10	11	12
13	14	15	16	17	18	19
20	21	22	23	24	25	26
27	28	29	30	31		

22
sunday

November

23
monday

24
tuesday
First Quarter ◐

25
wednesday

26
thursday
Thanksgiving Day

27
friday

28
saturday

29
sunday

November

s	m	t	w	t	f	s
1	2	3	4	5	6	7
8	9	10	11	12	13	14
15	16	17	18	19	20	21
22	23	24	25	26	27	28
29	30					

December

s	m	t	w	t	f	s
		1	2	3	4	5
6	7	8	9	10	11	12
13	14	15	16	17	18	19
20	21	22	23	24	25	26
27	28	29	30	31		

You should be thankful for everything at all times. Realize that all power to think, and speak, and act comes from God, and that He is with you now, guiding and inspiring you.

— Paramahansa Yogananda

Yosemite valley, California   Photograph by Wendy Kaveney, www.throughwendyslens.com

Keep the undercurrent of happiness, the secret river of joy, flowing beneath the sands of your various thoughts and the rocky soil of your hard trials.

– Paramahansa Yogananda

Ohiopyle State Park, Pennsylvania   Photograph by Larry Davis / Profotos

30
monday

St. Andrew's Day (Scot.)

1
tuesday

Full Moon ○

2
wednesday

3
thursday

4
friday

December

s	m	t	w	t	f	s
		1	2	3	4	5
6	7	8	9	10	11	12
13	14	15	16	17	18	19
20	21	22	23	24	25	26
27	28	29	30	31		

January 2010

s	m	t	w	t	f	s
					1	2
3	4	5	6	7	8	9
10	11	12	13	14	15	16
17	18	19	20	21	22	23
24/31	25	26	27	28	29	30

5
saturday

6
sunday

December

7
monday

8
tuesday
Last Quarter ◑

9
wednesday

10
thursday

11
friday

12
saturday
Hanukkah

13
sunday

December

s	m	t	w	t	f	s
		1	2	3	4	5
6	7	8	9	10	11	12
13	14	15	16	17	18	19
20	21	22	23	24	25	26
27	28	29	30	31		

January 2010

s	m	t	w	t	f	s
					1	2
3	4	5	6	7	8	9
10	11	12	13	14	15	16
17	18	19	20	21	22	23
24/31	25	26	27	28	29	30

The God of the clouds, the God of the moon and the sun, the God who is templed in all creation is within you and manifests as peace.

— Paramahansa Yogananda

Mt. Shuksan and Picture Lake, Washington   Photograph by Jamie and Judy Wild

Come into the silence of solitude, and the vibration there will talk to you with the voice of God, and you will know that the invisible has become visible and the unreal has become real.

– Paramahansa Yogananda

Yosemite valley, California   Photograph by Wendy Kaveney, www.throughwendyslens.com

December

14
monday

15
tuesday

New Moon ●

16
wednesday

17
thursday

18
friday

December

s	m	t	w	t	f	s
		1	2	3	4	5
6	7	8	9	10	11	12
13	14	15	16	17	18	19
20	21	22	23	24	25	26
27	28	29	30	31		

19
saturday

January 2010

s	m	t	w	t	f	s
					1	2
3	4	5	6	7	8	9
10	11	12	13	14	15	16
17	18	19	20	21	22	23
24/31	25	26	27	28	29	30

20
sunday

December

21
monday

Winter Solstice

22
tuesday

23
wednesday

24
thursday

First Quarter ◐

25
friday

Christmas

26
saturday

Boxing Day (Canada, U.K., Aus., and N.Z.)

27
sunday

December

s	m	t	w	t	f	s
		1	2	3	4	5
6	7	8	9	10	11	12
13	14	15	16	17	18	19
20	21	22	23	24	25	26
27	28	29	30	31		

January 2010

s	m	t	w	t	f	s
					1	2
3	4	5	6	7	8	9
10	11	12	13	14	15	16
17	18	19	20	21	22	23
24/31	25	26	27	28	29	30

Christmas is a thought of spiritual grandeur—a realization that our minds are an altar of Christ, the Universal Intelligence in all creation.

— Paramahansa Yogananda

El Capitan, Yosemite valley, California   Photograph by George Ward

Think of the beautiful happenings of the last year.... Sow the good you did in the past on the fresh soil of the New Year, that those vital seeds may grow in an even better way.

– Paramahansa Yogananda

Barrington, New Hampshire   Photograph by Larry Landolfi / Photograph Researchers, Inc.

28
monday

29
tuesday

30
wednesday

Full Moon ○
31
thursday

New Year's Day
1
friday

December

s	m	t	w	t	f	s
		1	2	3	4	5
6	7	8	9	10	11	12
13	14	15	16	17	18	19
20	21	22	23	24	25	26
27	28	29	30	31		

Day After New Year's Day (N.Z.)
2
saturday

January 2010

s	m	t	w	t	f	s
					1	2
3	4	5	6	7	8	9
10	11	12	13	14	15	16
17	18	19	20	21	22	23
24/31	25	26	27	28	29	30

3
sunday

ACKNOWLEDGMENTS

We wish to express our sincere appreciation to the following photographers and agencies who contributed to this year's *Inner Reflections* engagement calendar. Following a contributor's name, in parentheses, is the month and a day of the week, or other description, where each photo appears.

AKM Images, Inc. (6/15)
Alamy (Cover)
AlaskaStock.com (1/26)
Peter Arnold, Inc. (8/17)
BIOS (8/17)
Denver Bryan (7/27)
Gay Bumgarner (Cover; Opening Photo)
Russ Burden (1/5; 11/16)
Jon Cornforth (11/9)
Daniel J. Cox (4/13)
Larry Davis (11/30)
Richard Day (6/8)
Mark and Leslie Degner (2/23)
Linda Drake (5/11)
Christopher Talbot Frank (6/1; 7/20)
Dennis Frates (3/2; 5/4; 5/18; 9/7; 10/5;11/2)
Tim Fitzharris (7/13; 8/10)
Jerry Ginsberg (9/14)
Darrell Gulin (4/6; 4/20; 8/31
Mike Grandmaison (7/6; 10/19)
Jaynes Gallery (10/26)
John Hyde (1/26)
Burt Jones and Maurine Shimlock (3/23)
Byron Jorjorian (8/3)
Wendy Kaveney (11/23; 12/14)
Kimballstock (7/27; 9/28)
Klein and Hubert (8/17)
Larry Landolfi (12/28)
Tom and Pat Leeson (9/28)
Cheryl Opperman (1/19; 2/2; 3/30; 6/22)
Don Paulson (2/9; 3/16; 8/24; 10/26)
Photo Researchers, Inc. (8/3; 12/28)
Profotos (11/30)
Rainbow (4/27)
Jorge Rodrigues (6/15)
Brian Luke Seaward (3/9)
Robert Servranckx (12/29/08)
Sojourns In Nature (12/29/08)
Therese Tusa (4/27)
George Ward (10/12; 12/21)
Dave Welling (2/16; 5/25; 6/29; 9/21)
Michele Westmorland (1/12)
Jamie and Judy Wild (12/7)

"THE IDEAL OF LOVE FOR GOD AND SERVICE TO HUMANITY FOUND FULL EXPRESSION IN THE LIFE OF PARAMAHANSA YOGANANDA....THOUGH THE MAJOR PART OF HIS LIFE WAS SPENT OUTSIDE INDIA, STILL HE TAKES HIS PLACE AMONG OUR GREAT SAINTS. HIS WORK CONTINUES TO GROW AND SHINE EVER MORE BRIGHTLY, DRAWING PEOPLE EVERYWHERE ON THE PATH OF THE PILGRIMAGE OF THE SPIRIT."

—*from a tribute by the Government of India upon issuing a special commemorative stamp in honor of*

PARAMAHANSA YOGANANDA
1893–1952

BORN IN NORTHERN INDIA IN 1893, Paramahansa Yogananda came to the United States in 1920 as a delegate to an international congress of religious leaders convening in Boston. He remained in the West for the better part of the next thirty-two years, until his passing in 1952. Reporting at that time on his life and work, a Los Angeles periodical wrote: "Yogananda made an outstanding cultural and spiritual contribution in furthering the cause of better understanding between East and West. He combined in a conspicuous degree the spiritual idealism of India with practical activity of the West....The centers he established, the great numbers he inspired to nobler living, and the ideals he planted in the common consciousness of humanity will ever remain a monument to his notable achievement."

Self-Realization Fellowship, the international nonprofit society founded by Paramahansa Yogananda in 1920, is dedicated to carrying on his spiritual and humanitarian work — fostering a spirit of greater harmony and understanding among those of all nations and faiths, and introducing to truth-seekers all over the world his universal teachings on the ancient science of Yoga.

Paramahansa Yogananda's life story, *Autobiography of a Yogi,* is considered a modern spiritual classic. It has been translated into more than twenty languages and is widely used in college and university courses. A perennial best seller since it was first published more than sixty years ago, the book has found its way into the hearts of readers around the world.

An introductory booklet about the life and teachings of Paramahansa Yogananda and a book catalog are available upon request.

SELF-REALIZATION FELLOWSHIP
3880 San Rafael Avenue • Los Angeles, California 90065-3298
Telephone (323) 225-2471 • Fax (323) 225-5088
www.yogananda-srf.org

BOOKS BY
PARAMAHANSA YOGANANDA

Available at bookstores or directly from the publisher

Autobiography of a Yogi

Autobiography of a Yogi *(Audiobook, read by Ben Kingsley)*

The Science of Religion

The Law of Success

How You Can Talk With God

Metaphysical Meditations

Where There Is Light: *Insight and Inspiration for Meeting Life's Challenges*

The Yoga of Jesus: *Understanding the Hidden Teachings of the Gospels*

The Yoga of the Bhagavad Gita: *An Introduction to India's Universal Science of God-Realization*

THE COLLECTED TALKS AND ESSAYS

Volume I: Man's Eternal Quest

Volume II: The Divine Romance

Volume III: Journey to Self-realization

SELF-REALIZATION FELLOWSHIP LESSONS

The scientific techniques of meditation taught by Paramahansa Yogananda, including *Kriya Yoga*—as well as

his guidance on all aspects of balanced spiritual living —are taught in the *Self-Realization Fellowship Lessons*. For further information, you are welcome to write for the free booklet, *Undreamed-of Possibilities.*

SELF-REALIZATION FELLOWSHIP

3880 San Rafael Avenue • Los Angeles, CA 90065-3298

TEL (323) 225-2471 • FAX (323) 225-5088

www.yogananda-srf.org

NOTES

2008

January

s	m	t	w	t	f	s
		1	2	3	4	5
6	7	8	9	10	11	12
13	14	15	16	17	18	19
20	21	22	23	24	25	26
27	28	29	30	31		

February

s	m	t	w	t	f	s
					1	2
3	4	5	6	7	8	9
10	11	12	13	14	15	16
17	18	19	20	21	22	23
24	25	26	27	28	29	

March

s	m	t	w	t	f	s
						1
2	3	4	5	6	7	8
9	10	11	12	13	14	15
16	17	18	19	20	21	22
23/30	24/31	25	26	27	28	29

April

s	m	t	w	t	f	s
		1	2	3	4	5
6	7	8	9	10	11	12
13	14	15	16	17	18	19
20	21	22	23	24	25	26
27	28	29	30			

May

s	m	t	w	t	f	s
				1	2	3
4	5	6	7	8	9	10
11	12	13	14	15	16	17
18	19	20	21	22	23	24
25	26	27	28	29	30	31

June

s	m	t	w	t	f	s
1	2	3	4	5	6	7
8	9	10	11	12	13	14
15	16	17	18	19	20	21
22	23	24	25	26	27	28
29	30					

July

s	m	t	w	t	f	s
		1	2	3	4	5
6	7	8	9	10	11	12
13	14	15	16	17	18	19
20	21	22	23	24	25	26
27	28	29	30	31		

August

s	m	t	w	t	f	s
					1	2
3	4	5	6	7	8	9
10	11	12	13	14	15	16
17	18	19	20	21	22	23
24/31	25	26	27	28	29	30

September

s	m	t	w	t	f	s
	1	2	3	4	5	6
7	8	9	10	11	12	13
14	15	16	17	18	19	20
21	22	23	24	25	26	27
28	29	30				

October

s	m	t	w	t	f	s
			1	2	3	4
5	6	7	8	9	10	11
12	13	14	15	16	17	18
19	20	21	22	23	24	25
26	27	28	29	30	31	

November

s	m	t	w	t	f	s
						1
2	3	4	5	6	7	8
9	10	11	12	13	14	15
16	17	18	19	20	21	22
23/30	24	25	26	27	28	29

December

s	m	t	w	t	f	s
	1	2	3	4	5	6
7	8	9	10	11	12	13
14	15	16	17	18	19	20
21	22	23	24	25	26	27
28	29	30	31			

2010

January

s	m	t	w	t	f	s
					1	2
3	4	5	6	7	8	9
10	11	12	13	14	15	16
17	18	19	20	21	22	23
24/31	25	26	27	28	29	30

February

s	m	t	w	t	f	s
	1	2	3	4	5	6
7	8	9	10	11	12	13
14	15	16	17	18	19	20
21	22	23	24	25	26	27
28						

March

s	m	t	w	t	f	s
	1	2	3	4	5	6
7	8	9	10	11	12	13
14	15	16	17	18	19	20
21	22	23	24	25	26	27
28	29	30	31			

April

s	m	t	w	t	f	s
				1	2	3
4	5	6	7	8	9	10
11	12	13	14	15	16	17
18	19	20	21	22	23	24
25	26	27	28	29	30	

May

s	m	t	w	t	f	s
						1
2	3	4	5	6	7	8
9	10	11	12	13	14	15
16	17	18	19	20	21	22
23/30	24/31	25	26	27	28	29

June

s	m	t	w	t	f	s
		1	2	3	4	5
6	7	8	9	10	11	12
13	14	15	16	17	18	19
20	21	22	23	24	25	26
27	28	29	30			

July

s	m	t	w	t	f	s
				1	2	3
4	5	6	7	8	9	10
11	12	13	14	15	16	17
18	19	20	21	22	23	24
25	26	27	28	29	30	31

August

s	m	t	w	t	f	s
1	2	3	4	5	6	7
8	9	10	11	12	13	14
15	16	17	18	19	20	21
22	23	24	25	26	27	28
29	30	31				

September

s	m	t	w	t	f	s
			1	2	3	4
5	6	7	8	9	10	11
12	13	14	15	16	17	18
19	20	21	22	23	24	25
26	27	28	29	30		

October

s	m	t	w	t	f	s
					1	2
3	4	5	6	7	8	9
10	11	12	13	14	15	16
17	18	19	20	21	22	23
24/31	25	26	27	28	29	30

November

s	m	t	w	t	f	s
	1	2	3	4	5	6
7	8	9	10	11	12	13
14	15	16	17	18	19	20
21	22	23	24	25	26	27
28	29	30				

December

s	m	t	w	t	f	s
			1	2	3	4
5	6	7	8	9	10	11
12	13	14	15	16	17	18
19	20	21	22	23	24	25
26	27	28	29	30	31	

2009

January

s	m	t	w	t	f	s
				1	2	3
4	5	6	7	8	9	10
11	12	13	14	15	16	17
18	19	20	21	22	23	24
25	26	27	28	29	30	31

February

s	m	t	w	t	f	s
1	2	3	4	5	6	7
8	9	10	11	12	13	14
15	16	17	18	19	20	21
22	23	24	25	26	27	28

March

s	m	t	w	t	f	s
1	2	3	4	5	6	7
8	9	10	11	12	13	14
15	16	17	18	19	20	21
22	23	24	25	26	27	28
29	30	31				

April

s	m	t	w	t	f	s
			1	2	3	4
5	6	7	8	9	10	11
12	13	14	15	16	17	18
19	20	21	22	23	24	25
26	27	28	29	30		

May

s	m	t	w	t	f	s
					1	2
3	4	5	6	7	8	9
10	11	12	13	14	15	16
17	18	19	20	21	22	23
24/31	25	26	27	28	29	30

June

s	m	t	w	t	f	s
	1	2	3	4	5	6
7	8	9	10	11	12	13
14	15	16	17	18	19	20
21	22	23	24	25	26	27
28	29	30				

July

s	m	t	w	t	f	s
			1	2	3	4
5	6	7	8	9	10	11
12	13	14	15	16	17	18
19	20	21	22	23	24	25
26	27	28	29	30	31	

August

s	m	t	w	t	f	s
						1
2	3	4	5	6	7	8
9	10	11	12	13	14	15
16	17	18	19	20	21	22
23/30	24/31	25	26	27	28	29

September

s	m	t	w	t	f	s
		1	2	3	4	5
6	7	8	9	10	11	12
13	14	15	16	17	18	19
20	21	22	23	24	25	26
27	28	29	30			

October

s	m	t	w	t	f	s
				1	2	3
4	5	6	7	8	9	10
11	12	13	14	15	16	17
18	19	20	21	22	23	24
25	26	27	28	29	30	31

November

s	m	t	w	t	f	s
1	2	3	4	5	6	7
8	9	10	11	12	13	14
15	16	17	18	19	20	21
22	23	24	25	26	27	28
29	30					

December

s	m	t	w	t	f	s
		1	2	3	4	5
6	7	8	9	10	11	12
13	14	15	16	17	18	19
20	21	22	23	24	25	26
27	28	29	30	31		

January

Sunday	Monday	Tuesday	Wednesday	Thursday	Friday	Saturday
				1	2	3
4	5	6	7	8	9	10
11	12	13	14	15	16	17
18	19	20	21	22	23	24
25	26	27	28	29	30	31

Jan 1 New Year's Day
Jan 2 Day After New Year's Day (N.Z.) / Bank Holiday (Scot.)
Jan 5 Paramahansa Yogananda's Birthday
Jan 19 Martin Luther King, Jr's. Birthday (Observed)
Jan 26 Australia Day (Aus.)

February

Sunday	Monday	Tuesday	Wednesday	Thursday	Friday	Saturday
1	2	3	4	5	6	7
8	9	10	11	12	13	14
15	16	17	18	19	20	21
22	23	24	25	26	27	28

Feb 6 Waitangi Day (N.Z.)
Feb 12 Lincoln's Birthday
Feb 14 St.Valentine's Day (U.S., Canada, and U.K.)
Feb 16 Washington's Birthday (Observed) / Presidents' Day

March

Sunday	Monday	Tuesday	Wednesday	Thursday	Friday	Saturday
1	2	3	4	5	6	7
8	9	10	11	12	13	14
15	16	17	18	19	20	21
22	23	24	25	26	27	28
29	30	31				

Mar 1 St. David's Day (Wales)
Mar 7 Paramahansa Yogananda's Mahasamadhi
Mar 8 Daylight Saving Begins (U.S. & Canada)
Mar 9 Sri Yukteswar's Mahasamadhi
Mar 17 St. Patrick's Day
Mar 20 Vernal Equinox
Mar 22 Mothering Sunday (Eng.)
Mar 29 Daylight Saving Begins (U.K. & European Union)

April

Sunday	Monday	Tuesday	Wednesday	Thursday	Friday	Saturday
			1	2	3	4
5	6	7	8	9	10	11
12	13	14	15	16	17	18
19	20	21	22	23	24	25
26	27	28	29	30		

Apr 9 Passover Begins
Apr 10 Good Friday
Apr 12 Easter Sunday
Apr 13 Easter Monday (All except U.S. and Scot.)
Apr 23 St. George's Day (Eng.)
Apr 25 ANZAC Day (Aus. and N.Z.)

May

Sunday	Monday	Tuesday	Wednesday	Thursday	Friday	Saturday
					1	2
3	4	5	6	7	8	9
10	11	12	13	14	15	16
17	18	19	20	21	22	23
24	25	26	27	28	29	30
31						

May 4 May Day Bank Holiday (U.K. and Scot.)
May 7 National Day of Prayer
May 10 Sri Yukteswar's Birthday
May 10 Mother's Day (U.S., Canada, Aus., and N.Z.)
May 18 Victoria Day (Canada)
May 25 Memorial Day
May 25 Spring Bank Holiday (U.K. and Scot.)

June

Sunday	Monday	Tuesday	Wednesday	Thursday	Friday	Saturday
	1	2	3	4	5	6
7	8	9	10	11	12	13
14	15	16	17	18	19	20
21	22	23	24	25	26	27
28	29	30				

June 1 Queen's Birthday (N.Z.)
June 8 Queen's Birthday (Aus.)
June 21 Summer Solstice
June 21 Father's Day (U.S, Canada, and U.K.)

July

Sunday	Monday	Tuesday	Wednesday	Thursday	Friday	Saturday
			1	2	3	4
5	6	7	8	9	10	11
12	13	14	15	16	17	18
19	20	21	22	23	24	25
26	27	28	29	30	31	

July 1 Canada Day (Canada)
July 4 Independence Day
July 25 Mahavatar Babaji Commemoration Day

August

Sunday	Monday	Tuesday	Wednesday	Thursday	Friday	Saturday
						1
2	3	4	5	6	7	8
9	10	11	12	13	14	15
16	17	18	19	20	21	22
23	24	25	26	27	28	29
30	31					

Aug 3 Summer Bank Holiday (Scot.)
Aug 14 Janmashtami
Aug 31 Summer Bank Holiday (U.K. except Scot.)

September

Sunday	Monday	Tuesday	Wednesday	Thursday	Friday	Saturday
		1	2	3	4	5
6	7	8	9	10	11	12
13	14	15	16	17	18	19
20	21	22	23	24	25	26
27	28	29	30			

Sep 6 Father's Day (Aus. and N.Z.)
Sep 7 Labor Day (U.S. and Canada)
Sep 19 Rosh Hashanah
Sep 22 Autumnal Equinox
Sep 26 Lahiri Mahasaya's Mahasamadhi
Sep 28 Yom Kippur
Sep 30 Lahiri Mahasaya's Birthday

October

Sunday	Monday	Tuesday	Wednesday	Thursday	Friday	Saturday
				1	2	3
4	5	6	7	8	9	10
11	12	13	14	15	16	17
18	19	20	21	22	23	24
25	26	27	28	29	30	31

Oct 12 Columbus Day
Oct 12 Thanksgiving Day (Canada)
Oct 26 Labour Day (N.Z.)
Oct 31 Halloween (U.S., Canada, and U.K.)

November

Sunday	Monday	Tuesday	Wednesday	Thursday	Friday	Saturday
1	2	3	4	5	6	7
8	9	10	11	12	13	14
15	16	17	18	19	20	21
22	23	24	25	26	27	28
29	30					

Nov 1 Daylight Saving Ends (U.S. and Canada)
Nov 3 General Election Day
Nov 5 Guy Fawkes Day (Eng.)
Nov 8 Remembrance Sunday (U.K.)
Nov 11 Veterans Day
Nov 11 Remembrance Day (Canada)
Nov 26 Thanksgiving Day
Nov 30 St. Andrew's Day (Scot.)

December

Sunday	Monday	Tuesday	Wednesday	Thursday	Friday	Saturday
		1	2	3	4	5
6	7	8	9	10	11	12
13	14	15	16	17	18	19
20	21	22	23	24	25	26
27	28	29	30	31		

Dec 12 Hanukkah
Dec 21 Winter Solstice
Dec 25 Christmas
Dec 26 Boxing Day (Canada, U.K., Aus., and N.Z.)

NOTES